D1415132

CHAMPIONS
OF
SCIENCE

BY
JOHN HUDSON TINER

Master
Books

First printing: March 2000

ISBN: 0-89051-280-9
Library of Congress Number: 99-67330

Cover by Farewell Communications

Printed in the United States of America

Please visit our website for other great titles:
www.masterbooks.net

For information regarding publicity for author interviews, contact Dianna Fletcher at (870) 438-5288.

This book is dedicated
to
Lenon and Marie Dawson.

CONTENTS

1

THE DAWN OF MODERN SCIENCE

S uppose a teacher of the 1500s asked a scientific question. Students did not solve it by experiments. Instead, they hurried to find the answer in ancient Greek books. If the answer they found disagreed with what they observed, then the error was with their eyes and not in the ancient books.

Changing this attitude and establishing modern science took exceptional skill and personal courage. Overcoming the powerful authority of the long-dead Greeks was an enormous challenge. One of those who took up the challenge was Copernicus.

The great astronomer Nicolaus Copernicus was born in 1473 in Poland. He was the son of a wealthy family. He was able to attend the best schools to prepare him for any profession he chose. Would he be a scientist? At the University of Krakow in Poland, he took courses in mathematics, philosophy, and astronomy. Would he be a scholar? He traveled to Italy to study literature at Bologna. Would he be a doctor? He studied medicine at Padua, Italy. What about becoming a lawyer? He studied law at the University of Ferrara, Italy.

Copernicus could have been a doctor, lawyer, or held a high government post. Instead, he served as a bishop's private physician. He faithfully devoted most of his time to church work.

Nicolaus
Copernicus

In his spare time, Copernicus studied astronomy. One practical reason to study astronomy was to produce an accurate calendar. A calendar was important to merchants, churchgoers, and country people. Most calendars listed more than days, weeks, and months. The extended calendars were known as almanacs, from an Arab word meaning a calendar of the heavens.

Almanacs contained information such as times of sunrise, sunset, full moon, and holidays. In addition, they usually contained remembrances of historical events, riddles, pithy sayings, simple home remedies for sickness or injuries, and other tips for a better life. A well-written almanac would be used every day, the year around.

Farmers used almanacs to plan when to plant and harvest crops. Governments and church leaders relied on calendars and almanacs to mark off holidays and special events. Some communities planned a harvest festival on the first full moon in October.

How does a person who makes a calendar or almanac know when the events will occur? The Bible says that God made the sun, moon, and stars. In Genesis 1:14 the Bible reads: "And God said, 'Let there be lights in the expanse of the sky to separate the day from the night, and let them serve as signs to mark seasons and days and years.' "

Astronomers calculated orbits of planets to predict their positions and forecast celestial events such as eclipses. A skilled astronomer could calculate the position of sun, moon, and planets for a date far in the future. Almanacs and calendars were built from this information.

Astronomers today use computers to calculate celestial events. Five hundred years ago, Copernicus had to make these difficult calculations with pen and paper. The calculations were not easy and were prone to error. One problem was the complicated way that Greek astronomers viewed the planetary system.

Aristotle, an important Greek scholar, wrote about astronomy. Few people dared to question his ideas. What Aristotle said settled the matter. He put a motionless earth at the very center of the universe. Everything in the sky revolved around our planet. He believed the circle to be the perfect figure. Aristotle reasoned that heavenly bodies were perfect, so their paths must be perfectly circular. The sun, moon, and each of the five visible planets were carried around in circular orbits.

Copernicus, like astronomers after Aristotle, noticed a puzzling change in the paths of the planets Mars, Jupiter, and Saturn. Every once in a while these planets slowed in their forward orbit. They stopped, made a backward loop and then went forward again.

Greek astronomers struggled to preserve Aristotle's plan for the heavens. One Greek astronomer, Ptolemy, succeeded in explaining the backward loops of Mars, Jupiter, and Saturn. He used a combination of smaller circles looping around larger circles. In all, his complex system employed 70 circles.

Copernicus could not believe that tracking the sun, moon, and five planets would take 70 circles.

To simplify matters, Copernicus made two assumptions: the earth rotates on its axis every 24 hours, and the sun is at the center of the planetary system.

The sun-centered model of the solar system explained the backward loops of Mars, Jupiter, and Saturn. Those planets orbited further from the sun than the earth. As the earth overtook them, they fell behind. They seemed to travel in reverse. Mars orbited the sun in two years but the earth sped around in only one year. When earth passed Mars, it seemed to fall backwards.

Copernicus explained it with an example. Imagine a speedy horse passing a slower cart. Both are going in the same direction. The horse overtakes the cart and passes it. To the rider on the horse, the cart appears to fall behind.

Copernicus worked out his system in full mathematical detail. He summarized his ideas in a short, handwritten manuscript. He sent it around to his friends and fellow scientists. He still used circles to describe planetary motions. Also, he didn't entirely eliminate all the extra, small circles that Ptolemy used. However, Copernicus' ideas did make easier the prediction of celestial events.

At first, Copernicus recommended his system only because it was quicker and more accurate. Then he noticed that his sun-centered planetary system could explain observations that baffled the Greeks. For instance, Mars changed in brightness. During a period of about two years, it faded from a bright red object to a much dimmer light. Why?

The earth-centered planetary system of Greek science offered no explanation. According to Aristotle, Mars circled the earth. It should have been equally bright the year around.

Copernicus' system gave a reason. Mars and Earth both traveled around the sun. They orbited at different speeds. Sometimes their orbits brought them closer together. Mars looked brighter. At other times, their orbits drew them farther apart. From the greater distance, Mars looked dimmer.

Copernicus spent many years gathering evidence for his sun-centered theory. He observed the planets carefully and made detailed calculations. He improved the original handwritten manuscript. He called the new book *On the Revolution of the Celestial Sphere*.

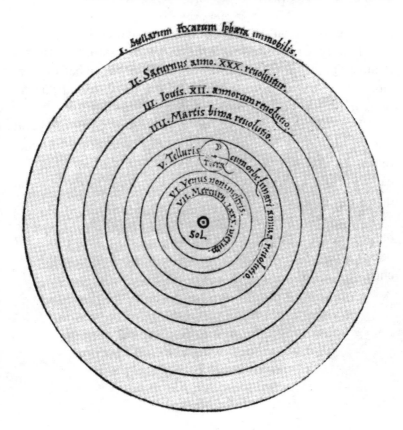

A diagram of Copernicus' sun-centered system of the universe, from his book in 1543.

Friends encouraged Copernicus to publish the book but he hesitated. People believed that everything had a natural place. Flame rose to the sky because that was its natural place. Rocks fell to earth because that was their natural place. Kings sat on their thrones because that was their natural place.

Rulers did not encourage new ideas. Suppose astronomers removed the earth from its natural place as the center of the universe. People might think a king didn't belong on his throne at the center of the kingdom. New ideas led to unrest. Those in power punished authors of books that caused problems.

Finally, Copernicus took the dangerous step. He sent his manuscript to a printer. On May 24, 1543, he lay in bed desperately ill. The first copy of the book arrived. A friend put the book in his hands. Copernicus died that same day.

In his book, Copernicus gave evidence that the sun and not the earth was at the center of the planetary system. He correctly stated that the earth is a globe that spins on its axis. The earth and all the planets revolve around the sun. The moon alone orbits the earth.

The honor of writing the first modern book on science belongs to Copernicus. The publication of *On the Revolution* began a revolution not only in astronomy but also in all science.

2

THE IRON FIST OF ARISTOTLE

T he ancient world produced many great thinkers. Most fell short of what it takes to be good scientists. Some appealed to reason alone without doing experiments. Others were mystics. They based their pronouncements on the alignment of stars or other chance events. Still others let superstition rule their lives. Aristotle rose above the general superstition of his time.

Aristotle was born in Macedonia in 384 B.C. Macedonia was a Greek providence about 300 miles north of Athens. Aristotle grew up in a world where people believed that the actions of spiteful gods controlled their lives. If you looked too closely at the world or asked too many questions, these petty gods might punish you.

His father was a doctor. When the young Aristotle became 17 years old, his father sent him to school at Plato's Academy. Scholars considered this school in Athens the best in the world.

Macedonia and Athens were not friendly with one another. However, Plato recognized in Aristotle a person who put a desire to learn above politics. He welcomed the student from Macedonia. At the academy, Plato taught that it was all right to ask questions. Aristotle learned to observe, ask questions, and use reason to form conclusions.

An earth-centered picture of the universe, showing Artistotle's four elements — earth, water, air, and fire — surrounded by the spheres of planets and fixed stars. From Raymod Lulls' book in 1523.

Experimentation, however, was not encouraged. Students came from wealthy families where slaves did manual labor. It was unthinkable for wealthy students to work with their hands to do experiments.

Aristotle became a teacher at the academy. He stayed in Athens for 20 years. He only left after Plato died. The academy leaders still remembered that Aristotle was a Macedonian. Without Plato to protect him, Aristotle felt it best to return home.

The change did him well. He married. On his honeymoon

trip, he spent carefree hours in the direct exploration of nature. Aristotle especially enjoyed studying animals that lived in the sea. His bride watched as he waded into the warm waters of the Mediterranean. He observed sea life and used a net to catch specimens for further study.

Scholars gave the name "fish" to all sea life. They believed all creatures in the sea had similar traits. Aristotle examined the things he caught and studied how they were alike and how they differed. He saw clear differences. For instance, some had scales and others had no scales. He began a classification plan that put similar creatures together. One of the key steps in science was to summarize and categorize information so it was easier to understand. Facts that applied to one animal were likely to apply to other animals in the same category.

He noticed that dolphins give birth to live young. This fact along with other observations convinced him that dolphins were not fish. They were mammals like horses and cows. He put dolphins in the same category as beasts of the field.

When he returned home, the king of Macedonia had an assignment for Aristotle. The king said, "You are to tutor my son, Alexander." Alexander was 13 years old. Although he was a strong-willed boy, teacher and student became lifelong friends.

When Alexander was 20 years old, in 336 B.C., his father died. Alexander became king of Macedonia. He was a brilliant military leader. He united the warring city-states of Greece. He overran the ancient city of Thebes and marched across the rest of Egypt. He founded the city of Alexandria as a major seaport in North Africa on the Mediterranean Sea. He marched east and took Mesopotamia, pushed into Persia and led his conquest into India. He became known as Alexander the Great. Today, military historians name him the greatest military general who ever lived.

Aristotle could return to Athens under the protection of his former student. Aristotle began a school there using money supplied by Alexander the Great. Aristotle called his school the Lyceum. His students gave it the name Peripatetic School. This word means to walk about. Aristotle lectured to his students while walking in the school's garden. He would pick up leaves, feathers, and other objects and ask his students questions. He encouraged them to observe and think about what they saw.

Aristotle wrote about 170 books. The range of subjects and the insights in his writings and lectures were astonishing. He expressed important ideas in astronomy, zoology, geography, physics, and many other subjects, including government. For instance, he collected the constitutions of many nations. Aristotle wrote a book about the systems of laws that govern countries.

Aristotle believed education was essential to the survival of a nation. He said, "All who have meditated on the art of governing mankind are convinced that the fate of empires depends on the education of youth."

In 324 B.C., Alexander the Great died of a fever in Babylon. He was but 33 years old. With the death of his protector, Aristotle again faced danger from jealous leaders in Athens. He left Athens and lived on an island in the Aegean Sea. In this pleasant location, he died a year later.

The center of learning moved from Athens to Alexandria. This city, near the delta of the Nile River in Africa, became the gem of ancient cities. For hundreds of years, it served as the intellectual center of the world. It even boasted one of the seven wonders of the ancient world — the 300-foot-tall lighthouse of Pharos. The books Aristotle had written, along with others he'd collected, became the start of a library at Alexandria. Soon the city had universities, museums, and the greatest library of the ancient world.

As the years passed, the Greek Empire declined. About 150 years before the birth of Jesus, Rome gained control of Greece and much of Europe. Alexandria fell into Roman hands in 30 B.C. It remained the seat of the most extensive libraries, universities, and museums in the ancient world.

The Romans made far fewer scientific discoveries than the Greeks. They did, however, put science and technology to work. The Romans were the master builders and great engineers of the ancient world. They built roads and ships, improved mining, and made useful inventions.

However, the Roman Empire crumbled. Alexandria fell to Arab conquest in A.D. 640. They sacked the city and carried away the books. Europe plunged into the Dark Ages. For about 800 years, from A.D. 650 to A.D. 1450, learning in Europe came to a standstill.

Europeans forgot all the wonderful gains made by the Greeks. Copies of Aristotle's books were unknown in Europe. Education became of little importance. The leaders of most countries could not read or write.

Charlemagne, one of the great rulers during this time, could neither read nor write. After becoming king, he saw the importance of an education. He opened schools throughout his kingdom for the promotion of reading, writing, mathematics, grammar, and Bible study.

Charlemagne gave himself the task of learning to read and write as an example for his people. He succeeded in learning to read. He tried to learn to write, but as a child his fingers had not learned the small muscle control needed to form letters. Despite his determined efforts, he never succeeded in doing more than signing his name. After he died, the small spark of learning he began died out. Many of the discoveries of the Greeks and Romans became lost. Books were few in number and very precious.

Slowly this changed. In the 1100s, European Christians came back from the Crusades with stories of the unusual sights they saw. Interest in learning increased again in 1295 when Marco Polo came back from China. For 17 years, Marco Polo had served as a roving assistant to the renowned Kublai Khan, ruler of China. Marco Polo saw impressive sights such as the summer palace at Xanadu. He also saw a country far more modern than Europe at that time. Kublai Kahn believed in religious freedom and did much to encourage science, art, and commerce. His people used paper money as a medium of exchange. He welcomed visitors to his court.

Upon his return home, Marco Polo told about his travels.

A professional writer listened as Marco described the many marvelous sights. Today, a book of wonder and excitement similar to Marco Polo's travels would be printed in the millions. Marco Polo lived before the invention of the printing press. Copies were written by hand. Although his book created a sensation among those who read it, only a few hundred copies were made. Before people could act on the opportunities for trade and scientific exchanges with China, Kublai Khan died. His great empire fell apart and it was no longer safe to travel overland to China.

Although routes to China in the Far East were shut off, trade and travel between Europe and the Arab world in the Near East increased. While the darkness of ignorance gripped Europe, the Arab world had flourished. The books from the libraries at Alexandria had survived in Arab hands. The books, including 50 by Aristotle, made their way from Arab hands into the libraries of scholars in Europe.

About 1450, Johann Gutenberg invented the printing press with moveable type. Gutenberg's invention lowered the cost of books so they became common. Ordinary people could own them. Because of the availability of books, people saw the advantages of learning how to read and write. Education became important again.

After the invention of the printing press, writings by the Greeks were translated into Latin and printed in great numbers. Aristotle's books were some of the first ones printed. Compared to the scholars of the Dark Ages, he seemed much better informed. People of the 1500s began to think of his ancient books as the final authority on scientific matters.

Aristotle had encouraged observation and clear thinking. Yet, those who taught from his books did exactly the opposite. They believed his books contained all the answers. Despite his own advice to observe and think, Aristotle became a dictator of science. Ideas in his books ruled scientific thought as strongly as a powerful dictator.

3

GALILEO AND EXPERIMENTAL SCIENCE

The great Italian scientist Galileo was born 21 years after Copernicus published his book that put the sun at the center of the planetary system. Galileo is best known for his observations of planets and stars in outer space. However, his researches into the motion of objects on earth were as important to science.

His first major discovery came while he was a 17-year-old student at Pisa, Italy, in 1581. At the insistence of his father, he was training to be a doctor. He began his day by going to chapel. Early one morning Galileo knelt and whispered his prayers in the dark chapel.

He arose to watch the lamplighter work. The lamp hung 30 feet from the high ceiling. The lamplighter pulled on a cord to bring the lamp over the balcony. After lighting it, the lamplighter released the lamp. The lamp swung back and forth in a wide arc. Each large swing seemed to take the same amount of time. Galileo timed its motion with his steady pulse and saw that he was correct. After the lamp's motion grew smaller, he timed it again. To his surprise, each small swing took as long as the larger ones.

Galileo returned to his room to try other pendulums. He discovered that by making the string longer he lengthened the time for it to make one back and forth swing. Making the string shorter caused it to swing back and forth more quickly. However, if the length of the string was kept the same, then pulling it slightly to the side or far to the side made no different. A wide arc took as long as a narrow one.

This discovery was a new one. The ancient Greeks had not mentioned it in any of their books. Galileo became convinced that observations and experimentation were the way to learn new facts. He began to question what the ancient books taught.

Galileo's teachers held Aristotle in high regard. Aristotle would have been aghast at how scholars used his books. It wasn't his fault that teachers misused his writings. Considering the number of books that he had written, the number of errors in them was very small indeed. Unfortunately, Galileo found that the scholars of the 1500s held most strongly to Aristotle's incorrect ideas.

For instance, scholars taught Aristotle's contention that any ball-shaped object would sink in water. Galileo tested his idea. He made spherical objects from wood, wax, and lead. Some spherical objects floated in water. Others sank.

Galileo often argued with teachers and students. They gave him the nickname "the Wrangler." Unlike Aristotle and the other Greek scientists, Galileo was willing to do experiments.

Greek scientists wrote that heavy objects fell more rapidly than light ones. A ball ten times as heavy as a lighter one would fall ten times faster. Teachers at Pisa repeated this claim. The cathedral at Pisa had a bell tower known as the Leaning Tower of Pisa. Because of a shallow foundation, the tower began leaning shortly after completion in the 1300s.

Stories sprang up that Galileo dropped balls of different weights from the Leaning Tower of Pisa. Both light and heavy balls struck the ground at the same time.

All objects fall at the same speed, Galileo concluded. Air friction caused exceptions. Objects with large surface areas, like feathers, fell more slowly. Galileo proposed that in a vacuum where there was no air resistance a feather would fall as fast as a lead ball. His critics said he could safely make that statement because Aristotle taught that a vacuum could not exist.

Galileo became a professor at the University of Padua. Students enjoyed his classes. He had to move outside for more room. Professors who lectured from ancient books found empty seats.

Until then, people believed that a moving object would naturally tend to slow. To keep it moving, a force constantly had to act on it. Galileo believed just the opposite. A body in motion would stay moving in a straight line. For his experiments, he built a track of hard wood and rolled highly polished bronze balls down it. He reduced friction to a minimum. His experiments showed that a ball would slow down, speed up, or change direction only when a force acted on it. A ball rolling on a flat surface does slow. The force of friction brings it to a stop. A ball at rest on a flat table would stay at rest unless a force put it in motion. This discovery became Isaac Newton's first law of motion.

Scientists believed that bodies in the heavens followed perfect circles, while objects on earth traveled in straight lines. Galileo showed that the flight of a cannonball from a cannon followed a parabolic path. Moving bodies could follow paths other than straight lines or circles.

In 1609, Galileo put aside all of his work on motion. He'd learned of an exciting discovery — the telescope. Hans Lippershey of Holland, a lens grinder, had put together lenses to make the first telescope. Distant objects appeared near at hand. Gutenberg's printing press contributed to the invention of the telescope. The main lens of a telescope has the same shape as a reading lens. More books meant more reading glasses. It was only a matter of time until someone put together the right lenses to invent a telescope.

Galileo received a letter from a student who told about the invention. Galileo realized the scientific uses of such an instrument. Although he had not seen one, he reasoned out its construction. He built a telescope the same day he received the letter. The main lens, known as the objective, was a convex lens with a long focal length. It formed an image by bringing light from a distant object to a focus. The eye lens was a concave lens. It was placed just before the image formed and produced a right-side-up image.

His first instrument magnified three times. He soon succeeded in making a 32-power telescope. It was vastly more powerful than any in existence. Because of the way he constructed it, the telescope gave right-side-up views of objects on earth such as ships far out at sea or distant bell towers.

Galileo was the first to turn the new scientific tool to the heavens. Everywhere he looked, he made exciting discoveries.

He looked at the moon. Galileo saw mountains, craters, plains, and deep valleys. The moon was as rocky and uneven as the earth itself. From the lengths of the shadows and the position of the sun, Galileo calculated the height of one tall mountain on the moon at four miles. Until then, no one imagined that the moon might have features like the earth. People believed that heavenly bodies were different from earthly objects.

Galileo examined the sun. (This is dangerous. In his later years, Galileo became blind. He'd damaged his eyes looking at the sun with a telescope.) He found dark spots on the sun.

He inspected the star group called the Pheiades. A sharp-eyed observer could glimpse 7 stars with the unaided eye. With his telescope, Galileo saw a swarm of stars. He counted 43. In the Milky Way, he detected an enormous number of stars. They were so faint and crowded so close together that the unaided eye saw them blurred together.

Aristotle taught that the sun, moon, and planets were polished and perfect. The moon was a smooth ball, the sun an unblemished sphere. Stars were fixed in number and location. According to Aristotle, the Milky Way was a misty cloud.

Galileo wrote a book about all of these discoveries: mountains on the moon, spots on the sun, and the starry nature of the

Galileo demonstrating a telescope.

Milky Way. He published the book *The Starry Messenger* in 1610.

Did Galileo see anything to support Copernicus? Yes. When he viewed the planet Venus, he saw that it had phases like the moon. Mercury had phases, too. The way the phases changed, from crescent to half to full, agreed with the idea that Venus and Mercury orbited the sun.

Scholars asked, "How can the earth move? It would run away from the moon."

Galileo's telescope showed that Jupiter had four large moons revolving around it. Jupiter certainly moved, but it didn't leave its moons behind.

Some scholars refused to look through the telescope. "These things cannot be. Aristotle tells nothing of them. They must be the fault of Galileo's glass," they argued.

Galileo made several telescopes and sent them to scientists throughout Europe. They soon confirmed his statements.

Jealous professors tried to discredit him a different way.

"Galileo is trying to prove that the Bible is wrong," they charged.

The charge was groundless. Galileo had studied both the Bible and the heavens. He found no disagreement in them. Even so, the professors worked through religious authorities to silence Galileo. They forced him to stop publishing his books for many years.

As the years passed, Galileo gathered information for his most important work. He published the book *Dialogue Concerning the Two Chief World Systems* in 1632. The book presented all the evidence for Copernicus' theory.

His enemies charged him with being a heretic. A heretic is a person who pretends to be a Christian but is an unbeliever. The charge was untrue. Galileo was deeply religious. He'd even written a book on religious matters. He believed that none of his theories dishonored any of the facts in the Bible. He only objected to those who tried to stifle investigations of scientific matters.

He was brought to trial anyway.

Many church leaders protested bringing the famous scientist to trial. After all, his disagreement was with the books of pagan writers rather than with Scripture. He was found guilty but given a light sentence. They did not send him to jail. Instead, they put him under house arrest. Galileo died in 1642 at his villa in Arcetri. By then, he was recognized as the world's foremost scientist.

4

THE COSMIC MYSTERY

Johannes Kepler lived during the same time as Galileo. Kepler attended the University of Tübingen in Germany and studied to be a minister of the gospel. He prayed to go wherever God could use him.

Shortly before Johannes Kepler graduated, the seminary at Graz had an unexpected vacancy. The school needed a mathematics teacher. They asked the University of Tübingen for their best student of mathematics. The university selected Johannes Kepler. Church leaders asked him to move to Graz. It was far from home. He had prayed to go wherever God could use him. Kepler put aside his plans to be a minister. Instead, he traveled to Graz to be a mathematics teacher.

As part of his duties in Graz, Johannes Kepler wrote a yearly calendar and almanac. Farmers looked at almanacs to see when it was best to plant their crops. They had to be certain they planted after the last killing frost. They couldn't wait too long. Grains such as wheat, oats, and barley needed time to grow, as do vegetables such as cucumbers and onions. An accurate calendar kept them from planting too soon or too late, so they would not face hardships or starvation.

Merchants who traded with people in faraway countries wanted to know when the roads would be flooded because of spring rains or blocked by winter snowfall. An almanac listed when seasons changed and predicted the onset of bad weather.

Traveling after dark was very dangerous because of thieves and highway robbers. Those who had to travel at night consulted a calendar to learn when they would have the light of a full moon shining on them.

While a student, Johannes Kepler had taken a class in astronomy, a study of the planets and stars. In the astronomy class, Johannes Kepler learned how to calculate when the moon would be full, when the sun would rise and set, and when eclipses would darken the sun.

Astronomy should not be confused with astrology, a false science. Astrologers tried to predict the future by looking at the stars. At first, they only foretold events important to an entire country. They would point to a planet passing a particular star and say the event signaled a disaster of some kind such as war. The word disaster means evil star. Later, astrologers began making predictions about individuals. A person would base decisions about what to do based on these predictions, which were known as horoscopes.

The astrologers stated their predictions in vague language and unclear meaning. A few successful predictions about the future caused people to forget the bad guesses. Astrologers could claim to be right more often than wrong.

In Germany at that time superstition and fear about the night sky gripped the hearts of common people and learned scholars as well. Astrologers used this fear to their advantage. One astrologer told his students, "Always predict disaster. It is certain to come true."

Johannes Kepler kept careful records of predictions made by astrologers. After several years, it became clear to him that astrology did not work.

He knew that the Bible warned God's people to avoid soothsayers and fortune tellers. The Bible, and not a horoscope, told Christians what to do. Jeremiah told the people not to fear the signs of the heavens, as the heathen do (Jeremiah 10:2). Kepler agreed. He said, "I fear astrology is nothing but a dreadful superstition, so unlike astronomy which is a true science."

Kepler's first calendar and almanac was very helpful for farmers and travelers. He was asked to prepare a new one each year. To figure sunrise, sunset, moon phases, and the positions of the planets took a jumble of 70 confusing circles. The calculations took hours. The problem left him red-eyed and weary. He scratched out page after page of calculations.

Several years earlier, Copernicus had proposed that the sun and not the earth was the center of the planetary system. Few astronomers took Copernicus' idea seriously. The new idea did make calculations easier. Kepler began using the sun-centered planetary system. He quickly embraced Copernicus' theory as the correct one.

In 1596, Kepler published *Cosmic Mystery*, a book on astronomy. Johannes Kepler believed in a harmony in the universe put there according to God's design. He believed scientists could discover the design. He said, "Human beings are an image of God. It is quite possible that we think in the same way as God in matters which concern the adornment of the world."

In *Cosmic Mystery*, he became the first well-known scientist to publicly support Copernicus. He did so 20 years before Galileo.

Kepler also solved a long-standing mystery about Copernicus' book, *On the Revolution of the Celestial Sphere*. During the latter part of his life, Copernicus argued that the sun-centered theory was an actual description of how the planets moved. Throughout the book itself, he made the same claim. However, in the preface at the front of the book Copernicus wrote that he advanced the theory only to make calculations easier.

Kepler discovered the truth. Because of his illness, Copernicus had put the manuscript in the hands of a friend. The friend, who saw it through the printer, feared persecution. He wrote the preface and signed Copernicus' name. This action weakened the impact of the book. Johannes Kepler set the record straight.

Despite his best efforts, Kepler's calculations fell short of predicting celestial events to his satisfaction. He needed recent observations of the planets. The ones he used were centuries old. The only person who could supply him with the needed information was Tycho Brahe, an astronomer who lived in far-away Denmark.

Tycho Brahe had been born in 1546 to a noble family. At age 14, he observed an eclipse of the sun. It impressed him that such a spectacular event could be predicted with such accuracy.

Later, he found that astronomers were not particularly happy with their accuracy in describing the motions of the planets. They constantly debated about the orbits of the planets. Some placed the earth at the center of the universe. Others, like Copernicus, placed the sun at the center of the planetary system. Tycho — everyone called him by his first name — believed the debate could best be settled if astronomers had better and more accurate observations of the planets.

Tycho's idea of first gathering data before forming a theory is an important principle of science. It is better first to gather facts than base a theory on speculation.

As a young man, Tycho had a terrible temper. Once, he and another student argued over the correct answer to a mathematics problem. To settle the matter they had a sword fight. During the duel, Tycho's opponent sliced off his nose. Tycho had a replacement nose made of gold and silver. He glued it on with wax.

Tycho became an astronomer and spent 20 years making careful measurements of the position of the planets against the background of stars. His goal was to measure planetary positions ten times more accurately than the best work then available. He was fortunate that the king of Denmark gave him a private island and all the money he needed to build an observatory, the finest in the world.

This was before the invention of the telescope. Nevertheless, Tycho's observations remained the best available for almost a hundred years after the invention of the telescope. No

Tycho Brahe (1546–1601), a member of the Danish nobility, plotted the positions of 777 stars with his new and accurate instruments. His nose was cut off in a youthful duel, and he wore a false one of gold and silver — discreetly left unnoticeable in this portrait.

astronomer had ever matched his skill or number of observations. Even today, when astronomers combine observations over

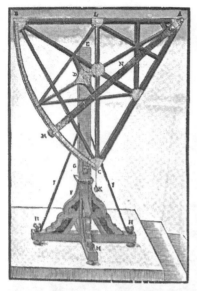

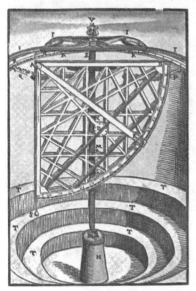

Tools fit for a splendid observatory. Tycho wrote a book about his instruments, illustrated with drawings of them, including the three above. The sextant pictured at upper left measured about six feet along one side. The huge equatorial armillary (top right) was about 16 feet high and had its own enclosure in Bahe's observatory. Observors mounted the tiered steps at the base to sight into the heavens along the plane of the great revolving ring. The picture at the lower right is of a 10-foot azimuth quadrant, accurate to 1/240 of a degree. Visiting scientists are reported to have jumped for joy on seeing Brahe's instruments.

several centuries, they continue to use Tycho's measurements.

His most careful measurements were of the planet Mars. Mars was visible throughout the nighttime hours and was easy to observe with the unaided eyes.

Kepler knew that Tycho was an exceptionally gifted observer. Kepler also knew that Tycho's mathematical skills were not great. When it came time to calculate the orbits of the planets, Tycho gave that task to professional mathematicians.

At that time, astronomers assumed that planetary orbits consisted of circles or combinations of circles. Tycho's observations were very exact. If the calculated orbit and his observations disagreed, then Tycho knew the problem was with the calculations. The mathematician Tycho employed could not produce an accurate orbit of Mars.

Because Tycho Brahe lived far away in Denmark, Kepler knew it was unlikely he would meet the astronomer in person. Instead, Kepler send him a copy of *Cosmic Mystery*. Kepler hoped that Tycho in turn would send a copy of his planetary observations. The great astronomer wrote a letter thanking Kepler and complementing him on his book. But Tycho had not yet prepared his observations for publication. Tycho would not let his precious planetary tables out of his sight. Kepler despaired of ever seeing the planetary data.

Kepler sighed. "I'll never be able to meet Tycho Brahe."

Then, because of his Christian faith, Kepler faced religious persecution. He was ordered from his home. He paid heavy taxes and sold all of his household goods at great loss. He fled to Prague, a city in what is now the Czech Republic. It turned out to be a stroke of luck.

Unknown to Kepler, the great Tycho Brahe had moved to Prague. Tycho, never an easy person to get along with, had disagreed with the new king of Denmark. Rather than fighting a duel, Tycho left the country. The great astronomer settled outside Prague and built a new observatory there. Kepler's book, *Cosmic Mystery*, had impressed Tycho. He invited the young mathematician to come to the observatory as his chief assistant.

He opened his observations of the planets for Kepler's use.

Tycho died suddenly in 1601. He left his treasure, his life-time observations of the planets and stars, in Kepler's hands.

Before he died, Tycho asked Kepler to calculate the orbit of Mars. Tycho asked, "What is the shape of the path that Mars takes in its orbit?"

Figuring the orbit of a planet is difficult. If Kepler succeeded, he would reduce the hundreds of observations of Mars to a single mathematical equation. Kepler worked on the problem for days and then years. Tycho's observations were particularly unforgiving. The accuracy of the data revealed the slightest errors. No matter how he placed the circle, no matter its size, he couldn't find a circle that fit Mars' orbit.

Finally, Kepler realized his error. He, along with all the other astronomers, including Copernicus, believed Mars traveled in a circle around the sun. Kepler had the astonishing idea that Mars' orbit must be a figure other than a perfect circle.

The solution took more than six years. Finally, Kepler had an answer that matched Tycho's observations. Kepler proved that Mars traveled around the sun in a stretched-out figure called an ellipse. An ellipse is like a flattened circle. Along its central axis are two points called foci.

Kepler swept away the 70 circles and replaced them with a single elliptical orbit for each planet.

Johannes Kepler summarized his findings in three laws of planetary motion. The first law states that the planets follow elliptical orbits around the sun. The sun is at one of the foci.

Kepler's second law states that a line connecting the planet to the sun will sweep out equal areas in equal intervals of time. An elliptical orbit brings a planet closer to the sun at one part of its orbit than at the other. A planet travels faster when near the sun.

The third law measures the distance to a planet by how quickly it travels around the sun.

In 1609, Kepler told about his discoveries in his book, *The New Astronomy*. He ended the book with a song of praise for the Creator. He wrote, "Thus, God himself was too kind to remain idle, and began to play the game of signatures, signing his likeness into the world."

Kepler did his work based on Tycho's observations before the telescope. In 1610, Galileo's discoveries with the telescope helped confirm Kepler's work. For instance, the four large moons of Jupiter followed the same laws as the planets, but with Jupiter taking the place of the sun.

Kepler examined Galileo's design for the telescope and saw that it could be improved. Galileo's telescope had a narrow view. It was like looking down a long tunnel. Kepler replaced the concave eye lens with a convex magnifying glass. This gave a wider view. The only problem was that the image was upside-down. For studying the heavens, this presented no problems. After the astronomer made his drawings of a planet or star group, he could simply turn the paper around.

As a child, Kepler suffered from an attack of smallpox, which damaged his eyes. He could not see very well, so he left exploring the heavens with a telescope to others. Once they made their observations, he applied mathematics to their data to calculate orbits and summarize the information.

In 1619, he wrote another book about his many astronomical discoveries. In the book, *Harmony of the Worlds*, he wrote, "Great is God our Lord. Great is His power and there is no end to His wisdom."

The third law predicted the distances of a planet from the sun based on the time it takes to go around the sun. The earth goes around the sun in one year. Saturn takes more than 29 years. Knowing this, Kepler calculated that slow-moving Saturn was almost ten times as far from the sun as the earth. Mercury required only 88 days to complete its orbit. Speedy Mercury was only four-tenths as far from the sun as the earth. For the first time, the vast size of the solar system became known.

With the three laws, astronomers could correctly predict the motions of the planets. Kepler's three laws of planetary motion became the foundation of modern astronomy.

Fifty years later, Isaac Newton used Kepler's work to develop the law of gravity. Newton said, "If I have seen farther it is because I have stood on the shoulders of giants." Johannes Kepler was one of the giants. One reason scientists so readily accepted Newton's law of gravity was because Kepler's three laws of planetary motion could be derived from it.

Johannes Kepler enjoyed great fame during his lifetime. After his death in 1630, his fame continued to grow. On any list of the greatest scientists, he is usually in the top ten. He was outspoken about his Christian faith. Often he wrote songs of praise to God in his science books. He urged scientists not to seek glory for themselves but instead give glory to God.

Johannes Kepler believed in a harmony in the universe put there according to God's design. He believed scientists could discover the design. He said, "Human beings are an image of God. It is quite possible that we think in the same way as God in matters which concern the adornment of the world."

What did Kepler think of his discoveries? He thought of his work as only another way of looking into God's creation. Kepler explained, "Together with the Holy Scripture came the Book of Nature."

5

A NEW MATHEMATICS

S cientists call mathematics the handmaiden of science. The tool of mathematics makes discoveries in other branches of science possible. Scientists such as Copernicus, Galileo, Kepler, and many others used mathematics to summarize vast amounts of data. Equations often bring to light discoveries that would otherwise be overlooked. Mathematics allows complex laws to be stated briefly and concisely.

Until the time of French mathematician René Descartes, mathematicians used the methods developed by the ancient Greeks. Most mathematical proofs were of a geometric nature. Although algebra had come into use, it was limited because scientists preferred visual pictures of geometry. René Descartes developed a way to combine geometry and algebra that made both more useful.

René Descartes was born in 1596 in France. His mother died a few days after he was born. He had not been given a name because he was so sick. At one point his family thought he had died. His nurse didn't give up, and slowly he recovered. Baby Descartes was named René from a French word meaning reborn.

He came from an old, noble family. Although his family was not particularly wealthy, he did receive the best education available. He attended a good boarding school, the college of La Flèche.

As he grew up, René Descartes continued to suffer from poor health. He convinced school officials that his health would improve if he slept late. He was a good student despite missing morning classes.

As René Descartes studied, he realized that the scientific knowledge of his day was not very reliable. René Descartes refused to blindly accept what he was taught. He asked questions and tested ideas. The more he studied, the more he doubted what he was told. He began to wonder what he could know for certain. Despite his misgivings, he stayed in school. He earned a degree in law, although he never practiced that profession.

At age 20, René Descartes dismissed formal schooling. He traveled to see what he could learn firsthand. For 12 years he explored Europe. He visited more than a half-dozen countries. He met with other thinkers who also questioned what schools and universities taught.

All of these travels took money. René had a small income from his family. He had to manage his money wisely. From time to time, he would join the army. This gave him a small salary. He never did see fighting.

In 1628 he settled in Holland to write about what he had learned. He chose not to return to France. He found the court life in Paris to be distracting and expensive. The people in Holland enjoyed more liberty than in some other countries, including France.

René Descartes began to think deeply about how one proves a statement true. Do you listen to experts? Do you read what a book says on the subject? Do you accept what seems reasonable? Or, do you learn from carefully controlled experiments?

Over the years, he developed rules for learning truth. He summarized his methods in a manuscript that he called *Rules for the Direction of the Mind*. He didn't have the book printed. He had put his thoughts in writing mostly for his own benefit. He put his methods into practice. He made several important discoveries in light, weather, and biology.

In 1633 he wrote his second book, *The World*, to report on his discoveries. In the book, he supported Copernicus' idea that the earth orbited the sun. Shortly before he finished the manuscript, he learned of Galileo's trial for holding similar views. René put *The World* aside rather than risk the same fate.

Four years passed. He wrote a third book, *Discourse on Method*, that he did publish. In the main part of the book, he discussed the nature of knowledge and the process of learning new information. This is a branch of philosophy. At that time scientists were called natural philosophers. Even today, an advanced scientific degree at a university is known as a Ph.D. The letters stand for Doctor of Philosophy.

In this book he used the famous phrase "I think, therefore I am." He expressed important ideas in the book. For instance, he said that it was not enough to posses a vigorous mind. One had to rightly apply it. *Discourse on Method* earned René Descartes the title "Father of Modern Philosophy."

René inserted at the back of the book three long articles about his scientific studies. For scientists, the most exciting part of the book was the third appendix. In it, he described his invention of analytical geometry, a new type of mathematics.

Geometry is one of the branches of mathematics and the oldest. The word geometry is from *geo* meaning earth and *meter* meaning measure. Geometry was well developed by the Egyptians. They used the principles of geometry to reestablish the boundary of fields following the flood of the Nile River each spring. Geometry ensured that the corners were straight during the construction of the Pyramids and large public buildings.

The mathematician who put geometry on a firm footing was Euclid. He was born about 325 B.C. Alexander the Great had died two years earlier and his kingdom was divided among four generals. Although Euclid probably studied in Athens, he wrote his book on geometry in Alexandria.

Euclid started with a number of definitions and basic assumptions. For instance, one of his assumptions was that the shortest distance between two points was a straight line. He arranged the book so that each result logically flowed from the basic assumptions. He supplied a proof for each conclusion.

Of all the works by the ancient Greeks, Euclid's book, *Elements of Geometry*, was the most enduring. In various translations, it remained the geometry textbook of choice for two thousand years.

Because geometry was so well developed, most scientists in Descartes' day depended upon it for their mathematical proofs. For many purposes in mathematics, geometry is clumsy and difficult to use. Algebra is a better choice to solve some problems.

Algebra is a branch of mathematics in which letters represent relationships between numbers. From ancient times, geometry and algebra were separate from one another. Geometry could mystify a person skilled in algebra, while algebra could bewilder a person knowledgeable in geometry.

René Descartes found a way to combine the two and make each one easier to use. He drew two number lines at right angles to one another on a sheet of paper. The number line running left to right became the x-axis. The number line running top to bottom on the

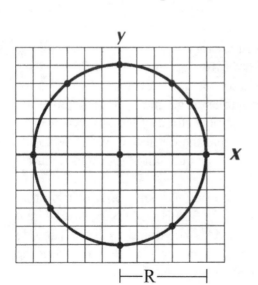

Descartes' circle graph.

page became the y-axis. Where they crossed, he called the origin. A pair of numbers could locate any point on the sheet of paper. One number was its distance from the x-axis and the other its distance from the y-axis. The point at the origin was $(0, 0)$. A point 3 units over and 4 units up was $(3, 4)$.

For the first time geometrical figures could be replaced with mathematical equations. For instance, a circle could be written as $X^2 + Y^2 = R^2$, with R the radius of the circle. The radius is the distance from the center out to a point on the circle. The superscript 2 means to square the number; that is, multiply the number by itself. For a circle of radius 5 units, the equation would be $X^2 + Y^2 = 5^2$; that is, $X^2 + Y^2 = 25$. Any point on the paper in which the X value and the Y value, when squared and added, equal 25 would be a point on the circle. For instance, the point $(3, 4)$ is on the circle because $3^2 + 4^2 = 52$; that is, $9 + 16 = 25$.

René Descartes' development of analytical geometry enriched both algebra and geometry. Proving the truth of a mathematical statement using geometry could be long and difficult. Doing the same proof with algebra was usually much easier.

The ancient Greeks and other mathematicians spent time studying conic sections. These curves include the circle, ellipse, parabola, and hyperbola. Cutting a cone at a certain angle makes each one of these figures. Cutting straight across the cone gives a circle and cutting at a slight angle gives an ellipse. Cutting parallel to the side of the cone gives a parabola and cutting parallel to the line down the middle of the cone gives a hyperbola.

A circle is the simplest conic section. Wheels and gears are circular. The circle has the property that every point on the circle is the same distance from its center. The circumference is the distance around the circle. The diameter is a line going from one side of the circle to the other by passing through the center. The ancient Greek scientist Archimedes proved that the number found by dividing the circumference of a circle by its diameter is always a constant. He named this constant *pi*, a Greek letter. He calculated the value of pi to be about 3 1/7, or as a decimal 3.14.

Pi is the same for any circle, regardless of its size. The distance around a small circle divided by its diameter is the same number as the distance around a large circle divided by its diameter. The division gives the answer 3.14. This is a handy tool for figuring the thickness of circular objects such as trees. With a flexible tape measure, the girth (distance around) a tree is easily measured. Dividing that distance by 3.14 gives the thickness (diameter.) For instance, a tree that is 63 inches around is about 20 inches through the middle (divide 63 by 3.14.)

The ancient Greeks believed the planets traveled in circles. Kepler showed that this was not the case. They traveled in elliptical orbits. The ellipse is another of the conic sections. Looking something like a flattened circle, an ellipse has two points called foci. Going from one focus to a point on the ellipse and back to the other focus is always the same distance. Some buildings have elliptical domes, which gives them an unusual property. Sounds made at one focus reflect from the dome and come together again at the other focus. Suppose a person stands under the dome at one of the foci and a friend stands far away at the other focus. They can whisper and hear one another as if they were standing side by side. Buildings with this special shape are sometimes called whispering galleries.

A parabola is another of the conic sections. It is like an ellipse that has been stretched so long that one of the foci is located infinitely far away. Galileo showed that cannon balls follow a parabolic path. Comets that come into the solar system from deep space follow a parabolic orbit.

Suppose a bright light is put at the focus of a parabolic mirror. The rays of light will reflect from the mirror in a tight parallel bundle. Searchlights have parabolic reflectors. Automobile headlights have parabolic reflectors. Placing the filament of a light bulb at the focus of a parabolic reflector directs the light far ahead along the road. A mirror with a parabolic shape has the useful property that it brings parallel rays of light to a focus. A parabolic mirror forms images of the sun, moon, or stars. The mirrors of giant reflecting telescopes have parabolic surfaces.

The last conic curve is a hyperbola. Hyperbolic curves are used in some navigation systems. Radio telescopes designed to receive X-rays from sources in deep space collect the X-rays with hyperbolic mirrors.

All of the conic sections were well known to the Greeks and carefully studied. As figures, their shapes are easily grasped. However, describing the figure in words is more difficult. For instance, a parabola is described in words as a plane curve formed by the locus of points equidistant from a fixed line and a fixed point not on the line. Writing its equation using analytical geometry is far simpler. The equation for a parabola is $y = x^2$.

René Descartes' invention of analytical geometry simplified science. The orbit of a planet or the flight of a projectile could be written as a mathematical equation. The 100-page appendix to Descartes' book turned out to be vastly more important to scientists than the rest of the book. René Descartes is today honored for his development of analytic geometry.

In 1649, Queen Christina of Sweden invited René Descartes to her court. She was a strong-willed 18 year old who wanted him to serve as her private tutor. He accepted the assignment. After he arrived, he learned that she wanted the classes to start at five o'clock in the morning! René Descartes always enjoyed sleeping late. He did some of his best thinking while resting comfortably in a soft, warm bed. The thought of getting up so early and facing the cold winter of Sweden repelled him.

Queen Christina made certain the teacher wasn't tardy. She sent palace guards to escort him to class. Only four months after moving to Sweden, René Descartes caught pneumonia. He did not survive the first winter. He died in 1650.

René Descartes had very simple and strongly held religious beliefs. He believed the laws of science applied to everything in the universe — except to God and the human soul. Descartes believed that God created the world and the laws of science. He believed everything functioned by the intelligent design of God. Much of his life was spent as a professional "doubter." Yet, he never wavered in his firm belief in God.

6

ANCIENT SCIENTIST, MODERN MIND

Archimedes lived more than 2,000 years ago. He was more modern in his thinking than the other Greek philosophers who liked to talk, observe, and reason but not experiment. Archimedes took a more hands-on approach. He did experiments and built scientific devices. If he could have been transported to Europe of the 1600s, he would not have been far behind Galileo or Kepler in his understanding of nature. He could have talked with them as equals.

Archimedes was born in 287 B.C., a few years before Euclid died. Archimedes studied in Alexandria under a mathematician that Euclid had trained. After his education at Alexandria, he returned to his home. He lived in the port city of Syracuse on Sicily, a Greek island to the southwest of Italy.

Archimedes became the foremost mathematician of ancient times. He calculated pi to an accuracy never before achieved. Pi is the number found by dividing the circumference of a circle by its diameter. Pi is used to figure the area of a circle.

The Egyptians and Greeks knew how to figure the area of ordinary figures such as triangles and rectangles. What of odd-shaped figures? How do you figure their areas? Archimedes found a solution by fitting small triangles and rectangles in them. This trick of replacing a hard problem into a series of easier ones led to triumph after triumph in the hands of mathematicians who came after him.

Archimedes investigated simple machines such as the lever and pulley. A pry bar is a type of lever. With a pry bar, a person of ordinary strength could lift a heavy weight. A few pounds of effort at one end of the bar pried up a stone weighing a hundred pounds or more. Was this getting something for nothing? He pointed out that the few pounds of effort had to be applied through a much greater distance. Overall, there was no gain.

Archimedes stated the law of simple machines: load times the distance the load moves equals effort times the distance the effort is applied. Simple machines are so ordinary and used so often, few people think about them. Yet, they make everyday life more convenient. A claw hammer for pulling out a reluctant nail is a lever. The rear wheel of a bicycle is a wheel and axle. A wedge for splitting wood is two inclined planes put back to back. Most wrenches are simple machines. Can openers, scissors, and many other tools use principles first described by Archimedes.

Archimedes told the king of Syracuse, Hieron II, that given a place to stand and a long enough lever he could move the world. Hieron challenged Archimedes to single-handedly pull a heavily loaded barge up on shore. A crowd gathered to watch. Archimedes attached a system of pulleys to the barge. He succeeded in dragging it ashore.

Next, Hieron II gave Archimedes a more difficult problem. The king had a new, golden crown. Had the goldsmith made it of pure gold as he claimed? Or, had he mixed in silver or some other cheaper metal? King Hieron ordered Archimedes to test the crown to see if it were pure gold. The king refused to let Archimedes file off a sample or do anything else that might mar its beauty.

Archimedes did his best thinking while soaking in his bath. One of his most important discoveries happened one day when he got in the water. He noticed that the level of water rose. He also noticed that he felt lighter. He seemed to float. Was there a connection between how much lighter he felt and the amount of water that his body shoved aside?

Suppose a barge is lightly loaded and more cargo is stacked on it. The barge will settle lower in the water. As it does it shoves aside some of the water. How much water? Experiments by Archimedes showed that the weight of the water the boat shoved aside equaled the weight of the extra cargo put on the barge.

Even objects that sank became lighter when dropped in water. He knew that lifting a stone under water was easier than lifting the same stone on land. Although the stone didn't float, it did weigh less underwater. Archimedes discovered the principle of buoyancy: The amount of weight a submerged object lost was equal to the weight of the water it displaced.

Archimedes thought of a way to test the crown of gold using the principle of buoyancy. Merchants weighed objects with a pan balance. A balance scale worked on the same principle as a seesaw. The scale had a balance beam with pans hanging from each end. Merchants put an object to be weighed in one pan. On the other side, the merchants added test weights of known value until the two pans balanced.

Suppose Archimedes put the crown in one pan and pure gold to balance it in the other pan. What would happen when he lowered the two pans into water? A crown of pure gold would lose the same amount of weight as the pure gold in the other pan. The balance scale would stay in balance under water.

What if the crown contained some silver? Ounce for ounce, silver is bulkier than gold. Silver takes up more space than an equal weight of gold. A crown of gold mixed with silver would lose more weight when immersed. It would be lighter. The crown in one pan and the gold in the other pan would no longer balance.Archimedes worked out all of this while in his bath. When he realized he had the solution he shouted, "Eureka!" *Eureka* is a Greek word meaning "I have found it!"

Archimedes now appeared before Hieron II and asked for the crown. He put the crown on one side of a pan balance. He added gold to the other side until it exactly balanced. Then he lowered the pans holding the crown and gold into the water. If they balanced, then the crown was pure gold. If the crown contained silver, then that side of the pan balance would come up.

The story is that his test showed that the dishonest goldsmith had mixed in silver to make the gold crown. Archimedes became world famous.

In 215 B.C. an army of Rome laid siege to the Greek city where Archimedes lived. For three years, his inventions helped the citizens of Syracuse keep the opposing army outside the walls. At last the Romans broke through the defenders and stormed into the city.

Marcus Claudius Marcellus, the Roman general, instructed his soldiers to spare the life of Archimedes. A Roman soldier came across a 75-year-old man drawing figures in the sand. He ordered the man to move along. The old man scolded him for stepping on his figures. The soldier did not recognize Archimedes and ran him through with a sword.

During his life, Archimedes searched for knowledge and truth. He saw the order put in the universe. We do not know to what extent he recognized the hand of God as the One behind that order. We do know that he was one of the greatest thinkers of the ancient world.

Archimedes in his bath. From Gaultherus Rivius' book in 1547.

7

EXPLORING MYSTERIES

B laise Pascal's father gave specific instructions to the tutor. "You are not to teach my son anything about geometry," Blaise's father said.

"Why?" the tutor asked.

"I want him to concentrate on other studies," Blaise's father explained. "He will have time enough for geometry after he is 15."

Blaise Pascal's came from a wealthy family but suffered the misfortune of his mother dying when he was three. His father raised Blaise and his two sisters. He saw to his son's education and hired tutors. At age 12, Blaise began drawing figures and studying their properties. Rather than taking a recess for play, Blaise secretly studied geometry. He proved that the sum of the angles of a triangle is always 180 degrees. When his father saw his progress, he gave the boy a copy of Euclid's *Elements*.

Blaise's father was interested in science. Father and son attended scientific gatherings in Paris. Blaise presented papers about his geometric discoveries. The scientists were astonished that a person so young could be so knowledgeable.

Late in 1639, Blaise's father was appointed tax collector for Upper Normandy. Pascal looked for a better way to lighten the drudgery of calculating sums of money. He built a mechanical calculator. He used a series of wheels that connected with one another. Each wheel had gears with ten teeth. A full turn of

Pascal's adding machine. In 1642 the French philosopher Blaise Pascal, 19 years old and tired of totaling up figures for his tax-collector father, invented the fancy machine (at right) for adding and subtracting. Its cylinders and gears (foreground) were housed in a small box (background). The wheels on the top of this box corresponded to units, 10s, 100s, and so on. Each wheel could register the digits 0–9.

one wheel would engage the next wheel and rotate its gear by one notch. Ten turns caused the next wheel to rotate once. Ten turns of the second wheel advanced the third wheel by one turn, and so on. The wheels counted by 1, 10, 100, and so on. Numbers were dialed by metal wheels on the front of the calculator. The answer appeared in little windows along the top. Pascal's machine could add and subtract.

Pascal constructed the first machine when he was 18 years old. He was a perfectionist with a stubborn persistence. He continued to improve the calculator for the next three years. He was finally distracted from his calculating machine when he read Evangelista Torricelli's book about air pressure. Torricelli was an Italian scientist who had assisted Galileo after he became blind. Torricelli helped Galileo study pressure of liquids and gases, and then did work in the subject on his own.

Ever since Galileo claimed that a feather and lump of lead would fall at the same speed in a vacuum, a debate had raged about whether a vacuum was possible. Aristotle had said, "Nature abhors a vacuum." Abhor means to view with horror. Scholars believed this meant that nature would avoid a vacuum.

Those who believed that a vacuum was impossible used a water pump as an example. A water pump starts by pumping air out of the top of the pipe. To keep a vacuum from forming, natures pulls the water up the pipe to fill the void.

Evangelista Torricelli proposed an alternate explanation for the operation of a water pump. Did a vacuum inside the pipe draw up the water? No, Torricelli said, pressure of the atmosphere outside the pump pushed water up the pipe.

How strong was atmospheric pressure? Torricelli noticed that the best water pumps could draw water no higher than 34 feet. He believed this meant that a column of water 34 feet high had the same pressure as a column of air that extended from the surface of the earth to the top of the atmosphere.

Rather than experimenting with water, Torricelli used mercury. Mercury, a liquid metal, is 13.5 times as heavy as the same volume of water. Instead of a tube of water 34 feet high, he could experiment with a tube of mercury 13.5 times smaller. He sealed a glass tube at one end and filled it with mercury. Then he upended the tube over a dish. The mercury drained out until only 30 inches was left in the tube.

Torricelli invented the barometer, a device that measures air pressure. However, those who clung to the old ideas still claimed it was nature's reluctance in allowing a vacuum that caused the mercury to rise in the tube.

Blaise Pascal built a barometer and devised a number of experiments with it. He agreed with Torricelli that air pressure acted on the mercury in the dish. The pressure of the air forced the mercury up the tube.

In one of his simplest experiments, Blaise Pascal measured the air pressure at the bottom of a mountain and again higher up the mountain. Pascal was not in good health, so he talked his brother-in-law into climbing the mountain and taking the readings. At a height of one mile, the mercury column had dropped about three inches because of the reduced air pressure.

"Can nature abhor a vacuum more at the base of a mountain than at its summit?" Pascal asked. "The pressure of the air is the sole cause of the mercury suspended in the barometer."

Pascal developed the principle that fluids such as water and air exert a pressure in all directions. A solid such as a brick only presses down on the floor. A liquid such as water exerts a pressure not only down but also against the sides of the container. Below the surface of the water, the pressure acts upward. This upward force was why the gold crown Archimedes tested lost weight when submerged in water.

Pascal invented the hydraulic press. This device has two cylinders with a liquid between the two pistons. Applying a force to the smaller piston exerted a larger force on the larger piston. The difference in the force depends on their sizes. If the large piston has ten times the area, then it produces ten times the force.

Archimedes had shown that one does not get something for nothing with a simple machine. It was true of the hydraulic press, too. A 5-pound force on the small piston produced 50 pounds of force on the larger piston. However, the small piston had to move ten times as much liquid.

For seven years, Pascal experimented with the barometer and pressure. Again, he gave up that subject only because another one of greater interest came his way. Pierre de Fermat was a French lawyer and amateur mathematician. He had been asked a question about probability. He couldn't figure out the answer and sought Pascal's help. The two men exchanged a flurry of letters, and in the process developed the modern science of probability. They expressed probability as a fraction between 0 and 1. If an event is very unlikely, then its probability is near 0. If it almost certainly will happen, then its probability is near 1.

Probability became a useful subject because scientists often deal with a multitude of particles such as atoms and molecules. These tiny particles make up every physical object. Atoms and molecules are very small and far too numerous to be tracked individually. Instead, scientists predict what the particles will do based on probability. The individual molecules of water or air bounce around in every direction. However, as a group their action can be predicted based on mathematics that Pascal and his friend developed.

Suppose a drug company develops a new medicine. Is it safe? How many test subjects should it be tried on before it is released to the public? The mathematics of probability gives the answer. Manufacturers test the quality of their product by taking samples from the production line. Probability allows the company to calculate the useful life of the entire production based on the few that are tested. For instance, suppose a company makes very expensive rubber hoses. The hoses carry oxygen to a patient in an operating room. As the hoses age, they become brittle and might develop cracks. When should the hoses be replaced? By studying a few samples, the company can recommend a replacement date.

Throughout his life, Blaise Pascal had been interested in

pursuing a better understanding of the Christian faith. At age 32 he had a frightening accident. While riding in a carriage, the horses bolted. The carriage was left hanging over a bridge. He was rescued, but the accident changed the direction of his life.

He devoted himself full-time to religious matters. He became one of the most important writers in Christian literature. He wrote, "Man needs a Savior if the world is to make sense." He found that Savior to be Jesus Christ.

His writings are noted for their logic and the passion with which he expressed his beliefs. Despite the important subject matter, his writings sparkle and can be read with pleasure. One of his famous sayings is, "This letter is longer than usual, because I lack the time to make it short."

Pascal's most important work in philosophy was a collection of personal thoughts on faith and human suffering. He had been frail at birth. He grew into a man of slight build and never enjoyed good health. He battled migraine headaches and painful stomach ulcers. When writing about pain, he knew about the subject.

René Descartes visited Pascal in his illness. They sat together as good friends and discussed their Christian faith. After Descartes left, Pascal wrote, "The heart has reasons which reason knows nothing of." By this, he meant that science and reason are not enough. God is above and beyond ordinary reason.

Blaise Pascal died at age 39. A servant found a prayer that Pascal had written. Pascal had sewed it into the lining of his coat so it would always be with him. "Almighty God, who gave your servant Blaise Pascal a great intellect, that he might explore the mysteries of your creation, and who kindled in his heart a love for you and a devotion to your service: Mercifully give us your servants . . . the grace to use [our talents] diligently and to your glory. . . ."

Despite his short life, Pascal made a difference in science, mathematics, philosophy, and as a Christian example. He is often listed as one of the greatest scientists and philosophers of all time.

8

THE INVISIBLE
COLLEGE

R obert Boyle lived in the 1600s. Although English, he was born in Ireland. Robert's father, the Great Earl of Cork, was one of the richest and most-respected men in the world. The Great Earl of Cork was a thrifty, hard-working, and religious man. He often ended entries in his journal with written prayers. He thanked God for blessing his enterprises. The great earl was concerned that his sons might become pampered and spoiled. To prevent this, he sent them to live with poor families.

The great earl explained, "I don't like to bring up my sons so nice and tenderly that a hot sun or good shower of rain would damage them, as if they were made of butter or sugar."

From the time he was six months old until he became of school age, Robert Boyle lived in the home of an Irish peasant family.

After Robert returned to his home at Lismore Castle, Ireland, his father hired tutors to see to his early education. The lead tutor told him about the exciting changes that Galileo and Kepler brought to science.

When Robert Boyle became older, he attended school at Eton in England. He became impatient with many of his classes. Following the lead of the ancient Greeks, science teachers still

This theatrical scene, painted in 1768 by English artist Joseph Wright, was called A Philosopher Shewing an Experiment on an Air Pump. *A similar experiment was first performed by Boyle. As air from the glass globe was evacuated, the lark was seen to pant, go into convulsions, and become motionless. A tenderhearted girl covers her eyes.*

avoided experiments. Instead, they simply looked for answers in ancient books. They taught by appealing to authority.

Those in charge of the school warned, "The teacher is not to permit any new opinions or discussions to be put forward."

Students had to study from approved books. Rather than books by Copernicus, Galileo, or Kepler, Robert Boyle learned geometry from Euclid, astronomy from Ptolemy, medicine from Galen, and logic from Aristotle. After graduation, Boyle took a long tour of Europe and then returned home.

Robert Boyle believed future achievements in science would come by experiments. His motto, "Nothing by mere authority," rejected the belief that he would find all answers in books by Greek philosophers.

To satisfy his interest in science, he moved to Oxford, England, to be near other scientists. Although he did not attend school there, he did meet with college professors and bright students. They discussed the latest scientific discoveries. He called the group his invisible college.

In 1657 he learned of a new invention, an air pump. Otto von Guericke of Germany built an air pump and provided a dramatic demonstration of air pressure. He had a hollow brass sphere made and cut it in half. He held the two hemispheres together and pumped the air out. The spheres clung together. A team of horses hooked on each side tried to pull the hemispheres apart. The strong horses could not separate the two parts. When Guericke opened the valve and let air swoosh back in, the spheres fell apart.

Did a vacuum hold the hemispheres together against the power of the horses? No, Otto von Guericke said. Pressure of the air on the outside pushed them together. They only came apart when he equalized the pressure by letting air inside.

Robert Boyle saw the air pump was an exciting scientific invention — as important as a telescope or microscope. He decided to experiment with an air pump. However, none could be bought, so he designed one and arranged to have it built. He explained to a friend at Oxford, "I wish to employ a bright young student to serve as an instrument maker."

His friend told him about Robert Hooke. "He's a deserving student. No one doubts his ability." Robert Hooke was an orphan who earned his way through college by waiting on tables.

Robert Boyle hired the young student. Robert Hooke proved to be a mechanical genius. He quickly took Robert Boyle's plans and built an improved air pump. Boyle's design improved upon that of Guerike's so much that he is usually given credit for its invention. The machine pumped the air out of a glass globe.

Would sound carry in a vacuum? Robert Boyle and Robert Hooke proved the answer by suspending a loudly ticking clock from a string inside the glass globe. They could see the watch mechanism moving. Once they removed the air, they could no longer hear the ticking.

Years earlier, Galileo predicted that without air resistance a feather and a lump of lead would fall at the same speed. Boyle and Hooke tested Galileo's prediction. They put the two objects in a long glass tube and pumped out the air. Then they turned the tube over. Feather and lump of lead fell side by side at the same speed

Pumping air out of a container reduced the air pressure. Robert wondered what would happen if he increased air pressure. Until then, scientists had experimented with solids and liquids. Robert Boyle made the first scientific study of air, a gas. Most people viewed air as a mysterious substance. Diseases, for instance, were blamed on bad air. If air followed laws like other substances, the fear and mystery surrounding it would be removed.

Air could be compressed so that it took up less space. Exactly how did pressure change the volume of a gas? Robert Boyle built an apparatus to find the answer. He made a large J-shaped glass tube. It was open at the top of the J but sealed at the upturned short end.

He poured mercury in at the top of the tube. It trapped a bubble of air in the short end. Pouring in more mercury compressed the trapped air bubble. He calculated the amount of pressure on the air by the height of the mercury column.

Robert Boyle found that doubling the pressure on the trapped air cut the volume in half. Three times as much pressure made the volume only one-third as much. The pressure and volume went in reverse to one another. If one increased, then the other decreased. This relationship between volume and pressure became known as Boyle's law. It was the first scientific law that applied to a gas.

Robert Boyle

As he finished his study of air, Robert Boyle became interested in chemistry. For the pioneer scientists of the 1500s and 1600s, pro-gress in chemistry seemed the slowest. Learning the composition of common materials was not easy. Predicting how one substance would chemically combine with another was even more difficult. Many scientists who were successful in other fields tried their hands at chemistry. They found chemistry a swamp of misinformation.

The false science of alchemy hindered progress in the true science of chemistry. Alchemists searched for a way to combine two ordinary substances and make gold. For instance, lead is heavy like gold and sulfur has its yellow color. Would combining lead and sulfur give gold? No, but one failure did not stop an alchemist from trying. Maybe he needed to add something else to the mixture. The yellow from eggs, for instance. Maybe they should mix silver with the lead.

Alchemists worked in secrecy. They refused to share their information. Their motto was, "Never reveal clearly to anyone what you have done." They didn't want to give away secrets that might make them rich. Alchemists repeated the same experiment time and again because they did not know others had tried the same procedure.

Robert urged his fellow scientists to report their experiments quickly and clearly so others might benefit from the new discovery. Even unsuccessful experiments would prove instructive, provided scientists learned from one another's mistakes. "List the compounds and the amounts used," Robert Boyle suggested. "Describe your equipment. Explain how to mix the compounds and in what amounts. State if heat is to be applied and how to separate the products of the chemical reaction."

Robert told about his experiments in an easy-to-read style. He didn't try to impress people with difficult language. A friend of Robert Boyle's read one of his books. "You make the study of nature seem so simple," the friend said.

Robert Boyle explained, "God would not have made the universe as it is unless He intended us to understand it."

Robert believed scientists should write clearly and publish their discoveries promptly. How could useful information be spread more quickly? He remembered the invisible college. Such a group would be perfect. Robert and his fellow scientists petitioned King Charles II. The King agreed to charter the group of scholars as the Royal Society. Its motto was the same as Boyle's: Nothing by mere authority. Robert and his friends became the first group of scientists to hold regular meetings. Other countries such as France began similar organizations.

Throughout his life, Robert Boyle looked for ways to improve science. He served on the board of directors of the Dutch East India trading company. Its ships sailed throughout the world. He suggested that each ship carry a science officer. The shipboard scientist would go ashore at the ship's ports of call. He would collect and report on the unusual plants and strange animals that he found.

As a Christian, he also urged the company to work closely with churches to send missionaries to carry the gospel around the world. Robert Boyle was a humble Christian who seemed to radiate the love of God to those around him. When he did good works, it was out of sight of those he helped. The great fire of London in 1666 destroyed most of the main part of the city. The fire left a hundred thousand people homeless. Robert Boyle worked behind the scenes. He saw to it that they received food, clothing, and shelter. Most people never learned who had helped them.

In the 1670s and 1680s, Robert Boyle was England's greatest and best-known scientist. Although his fellow scientists elected him president of the Royal Society, he decided not to take the office. King Charles II of England tried to reward him. The king offered to make him a knight. When Robert refused, he offered him a high government post. Again, Robert Boyle turned it down.

When asked what title he preferred, Robert Boyle said, "Mr. Robert Boyle, Christian Gentleman."

9

IT'S ABOUT TIME

A stronomy is the science that strives to learn about objects in outer space. For many people, it must seem a difficult task. Unlike other scientists who can do experiments in the laboratory, astronomers must study their subjects from afar. The fact that astronomers have learned so much about the heavens is especially remarkable.

During the early days of scientific discovery, Christiaan Huygens was one of the most successful astronomers. He was born in 1629 at The Hague, Netherlands. He lived at about the same time as Robert Boyle (born 1627) and Blaise Pascal (born 1623).

Huygens' father was an important person in the Dutch government. Christiaan enjoyed a good education, including instruction at home from his father and private tutors. Later, he attended the University of Leiden, one of the world's great universities. He studied mathematics and proved to be very skilled in that subject. However, astronomy captured his real interest.

His first views through a telescope disappointed him. The telescope lens acted like a prism. Rather than forming a single sharp image, the glass produced an image for each color. When he turned the telescope to a planet such as Mars, it was blurred by a series of red, green, and blue images.

Christiaan Huygens struggled to reduce the color fringes. Forming the image farther from the main lens improved the sharpness. A lens two inches in diameter needed to be in a tube at least 20 feet long. Making and using long and cumbersome telescopes took remarkable skill and patience. Christiaan Huygens, with the help of his brother, built a telescope 27 feet long. It quickly proved to be best of any then in use.

Christiaan Huygens turned to Saturn and spied a satellite of that planet. He calculated the size of his new moon. He was pleased to find that it was as large as the four moons of Jupiter discovered by Galileo. Huygens named his new moon Titan. In Greek mythology, Titans were a family of giants.

Galileo had looked at Saturn but failed to detect Titan. Although large, Titian is twice as far from the sun as the moons of Jupiter, so it is dimmer. Galileo did see a puzzling sight that he could not explain. His crude telescope showed Saturn with two handles, one on either side. Galileo couldn't imagine what they were. He came back to Saturn later. The mysterious objects had disappeared. What had Galileo seen?

One night in 1656, Saturn was favorably situated and the sky was especially clear. Christiaan Huygens turned to the planet. In astonishment, he saw that marvelous rings circled the planet. The rings of Saturn nowhere touched the planet. Christiaan Huygens solved the mystery. He also discovered why the rings are sometimes difficult to see. During part of Saturn's orbit, the rings turn edge on to the earth. They are so thin they seem to disappear.

Huygens learned that the lack of an accurate clock hampered astronomers in making precise measurements of astronomical events. The best clocks of his day were unreliable. Most kept time so poorly they had only hour hands. They were big, too, and took up entire towers at the city hall or in churches. Not only did scientists need clocks, but so did ordinary citizens.

As Europe came out of the Dark Ages, the number of merchants who lived in towns and cities increased. They hired people to sew garments, butcher meat, print books, make candles, and do other tasks. They expected their employees to put in a full day of work. The employees expected to have time off for lunch and to take breaks during the day. Everyone saw a need for accurate clocks.

The first clocks had no minute hands because they were so unreliable. The best of them still could be off by as much as a half-hour each day. Clocks kept poor time because there was no way to regulate them. A clock in a tower was run by a weight attached to a cord wrapped around a drum. As the weight fell, it rotated the drum and turned a series of gears. The gears either rang a bell or moved the hands on the clock face. The clocks needed to be regulated so that the drum turned at a precise rate.

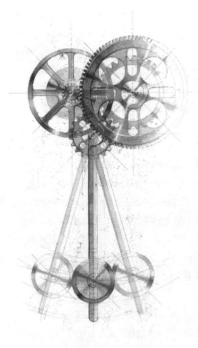

Huygens' pendulum clock.

Christiaan Huygens remembered Galileo's experiments with a pendulum. The pendulum swung back and forth at a regular interval. Could it be used to regulate a clock? Christiaan Huygens possessed a sharp mind and practical ability. With his own hand he built a clock capable of keeping time to the minute. Slowly falling weights on a chain kept the pendulum in motion. Instead of a clock tower, his clock was small enough to fit in a case. It could be a piece of furniture in a person's living room. Clocks of Huygens' design became known as grandfather clocks. For the first time clocks were accurate enough for minute hands. He presented the first working model to the Dutch government and described it in printed form in 1658.

By the early 1660s, Christiaan Huygens had become a famous scientist. He visited London to meet with England's great scientists, including Robert Boyle and his friends. The Royal Society of London met each week to exchange information about the latest discoveries in science. Christiaan Huygens attended one of their meetings and they elected him a member in 1663.

Huygens returned to Holland. King Louis XIV of France heard about the Royal Society. England and France were rivals. Louis XIV did not want his country to fall behind. He realized that science was important to the development of a modern country. He decided his nation should have a group similar to the Royal Society. He invited Christiaan Huygens to Paris and gave him money to build an observatory. He put Huygens in charge of starting a society of great scientists for France. In 1668, the Academie Royal des Science (Royal Academy of Science) began meeting. The members elected Christiaan as their first president.

While in Paris Christiaan made a much smaller timekeeper. It used the regular back and forth motion of a balance wheel to keep it on time. A tiny, flat spring attached to the wheel coiled and uncoiled at a fixed rate. For the next 200 years, all timekeepers used the principle of either the pendulum clock or the balance wheel watch to keep accurate time. Christiaan Huygens helped invent both designs.

Christiaan Huygens had very strong religious beliefs. By 1681, it had become difficult for him to remain in France and worship God. What to do? Christiaan had lived for many years in Paris. He made the difficult decision to leave the city. He had to give up his precious scientific instruments, say goodbye to his friends, and never again meet with the Royal Academy. He chose to return to The Hague where he could worship God freely. There he continued to make important contributions to mathematics, astronomy, time measurement, and the theory of light.

Christiaan Huygens is another example of one of the early scientists who exercised a strong Christian faith. Although science was important to him, he did not hesitate to put service to God first.

10

THE SCIENTIST WHO BUILT A CITY

C hristopher Wren, called "Kit" by his family and friends, was born in England in 1632. He was the son of a minister. He studied astronomy and mathematics at Oxford. He earned a Master's degree from that school in 1653.

His family was royalists. They supported the king during his losing struggle against Cromwell. Some of the members of his family were put in prison in the Tower of London. When the monarchy was restored, Kit Wren received appointments from Charles II, the new king.

Kit Wren was the friend of Robert Boyle, Robert Hooke, Edmund Halley, Isaac Newton, and many others. During the exciting years from 1650 to 1700, these people produced a large number of important discoveries. They would meet and discuss the great unsolved problems of their day. At one of these informal meetings, Kit Wren gave a challenge to Robert Hooke and Edmund Halley. He invited them to develop a mathematical equation that described the force caused by gravity. When Halley couldn't solve the problem, he took it to Isaac Newton. At that time Isaac Newton was not well known. His solution of Wren's challenge made him famous. One of Christopher Wren's greatest accomplishments was the good he brought out in others.

Christopher Wren's first professional position was at

Gresham College. He lectured on astronomy. Later, he taught at Oxford. There, at age 30, he put his mathematical skill to work designing buildings. People wanted buildings to have large, open spaces unmarred by support pillars. The building had to be structurally sound, too. It was a fascinating mathematical exercise.

By 1665 Kit Wren had become an architect. Designing buildings and overseeing their construction required an unusual mix of scientific and artistic skills. He had to be an excellent draftsman to draw plans and an able woodworker to make models. In addition, he had to deal with a variety of people. There were the builders such as stone masons, carpenters, glass makers, brick layers, marble cutters, lighting experts, and so on. He also had to deal with concerned citizens, business people, and politicians.

Kit Wren designed large public buildings, including hospitals and churches. The largest church in London was Old St. Paul's. Years earlier the abandoned building had fallen into ruins. It had been badly treated during England's Civil War. Cromwell had stationed soldiers and horses in the building. People had carted away loose stones. Charles II asked Kit Wren to restore the old church. Kit toured the building. It was in shambles. The decrepit walls threatened to collapse.

Kit didn't think the ancient gothic design would do for worship in his day. He explained, "Long ago, worship services were spoken in Latin. The congregation had little role in the services. It was not even necessary for them to see the clergy conducting the service. Things have changed. People want to see, hear, and join in the worship. The building must be spacious and open."

Kit Wren wanted to pull down the old building and replace it with a modern one of his design. The king and church leaders wanted to save the old building. Kit made ready to follow orders. First, he visited France to study its great buildings. He would strive to improve Old St. Paul's.

While he was away, the dreaded Black Death struck London. People fled from the plague in panic. Ten thousand people a month died of the disease. No one knew the cause, but they suspected the filthy conditions of the city helped spread the disease.

Kit stayed away until the disease ran its course. Shortly after he returned to London, a second disaster hit the city. A great fire burned through the old part of the city. It burned for four days and destroyed everything in its path, including 87 parish churches. The fire damaged Old St. Paul's beyond repair.

Charles II gave Kit Wren an awesome task. He was to design a new city, plan its public buildings, and supervise their construction.

For years, London had suffered terrible traffic jams along its narrow streets. Strong iron posts were driven into the ground near walls of buildings. People on foot would seek safety behind the posts to keep from being run over by horse-drawn wagons. Kit's design called for wide streets with ample room for pedestrians.

To control disease, he put in better drainage and a healthier water supply. To resist fire, he replaced wood and straw with bricks and stone as building material. He set aside land for parks and improved public buildings.

Kit Wren couldn't do all of this alone, so he called upon his friends in the Royal Society for help. Robert Hooke, who'd

London

been Robert Boyle's assistant, became his deputy.

As a Christian, Kit Wren believed that taking care of the city's spiritual health should be his top priority. He replaced the 87 parish churches with 51 new buildings. He designed each one for its space and surroundings. Each one was distinctive. Any of the 51 could be identified by its steeple alone.

To honor his efforts in rebuilding the city, the king knighted him in 1673. He was Sir Christopher Wren.

Finally, the city was on its way back to recovery. Kit Wren could give his full attention to building a new St. Paul's. He estimated that construction of the new church would take 35 years. No one who had undertaken the building of a cathedral had lived to see it completed.

Work started on the building. The years rolled by. Kit Wren married, had a son, and his son grew up. Work continued on the grand building. His son, Christopher, grew into manhood and had children of his own. Kit Wren was a grandfather. Still the

St. Paul's Cathedral

work continued under Wren's daily supervision. History swept by. Kings and queens rose to the throne and were replaced.

Kit Wren turned 60 years old in 1692. That year they had just begun on the great dome. It was still unfinished when they welcomed the new century. Now all of London could see the grandeur of St. Paul's.

Finally, in January 1711, St. Paul's was officially complete. Kit's son, Christopher, acted for him and assisted in putting the cross in place at its top. Sir Christopher Wren had seen it through to the finish. He made his first sketch when he was 33 years old. He saw the final stone laid when he was 79 years old. He had succeeded without betraying his Christian disposition. Some people who undertake a great task become obsessed with success. They become short-tempered with anyone who doesn't share their vision. They run roughshod over anyone who dares to disagree with them. Not Kit. Throughout it all, he'd remained cheerful, even-tempered, and polite.

While he built St. Paul's, he had experienced a full and warm family life and enjoyed the company of many friends.

Others approved of his success. They could not resent his genius when he gave credit to God for his success. They could not feel ill will toward a person with such a sunny disposition.

Each year, during the quiet time of winter in London, Kit would enter St. Paul's. He would sit under its great dome. In the church's quite and solemn atmosphere, he would spend time in prayer. In February 1723, he reflected on the happiness he felt. He'd lived a full and interesting life. He'd succeeded in building St. Paul's. He'd raised a family. He'd enjoyed the company of the greatest scientists of his times. God had been so good to him!

He returned to his home at Hampton Court. After dinner, he took a nap in his favorite chair by the fire. He drifted off into a peaceful sleep. At age 91, Sir Christopher Wren passed from the city he'd built to a city not made by human hands. He died.

They buried his body inside St. Paul's. The inscription on his crypt reads, "If you seek his monument, look around."